God's Perfect Gift
Love

Connie Weatherford

First Publishing

God's Perfect Gift - Love

ISBN 978-0-9853893-9-0
Copyright © 2017 by Connie Wilkett Weatherford

Published by
Goldfinch Oracles, LLC
113 N. 1st Street
McAlester, OK 74501

If you would like to purchase a copy of this book, please email the publisher at gwenniepoo@sbcglobal.net or find it on amazon.com.

The Publisher's aim is to produce books for the edification and building up of the Kingdom of God. The Publisher does not necessarily agree with every view expressed by the Author or interpretation of the scriptures. It is left to the Reader to make his/her judgment in the light of their understanding of God's Word by the Spirit.

Unless otherwise noted, all scripture quotations are from the King James Version of the Bible.

Printed in the United States of America
All rights reserved under International Copyright Law. Contents and/or cover may not be reproduced in whole or in part in any form without the express written consent of the Publisher.

Cover design by Gwen Titsworth
Goldfinch Oracles, LLC

DEDICATION

This book is dedicated

To the memory of all the women

Who made a difference in our lives.

Their spirit of giving will live

On through generations to come.

The Perfect Gift

It was the beginning of a new day. I thought to myself, as I smelled the aroma of fresh coffee brewing, felt the warmth from the fireplace, and relaxing in my favorite chair, 'It doesn't get any better than this!' Then, I remembered that three of my sweet little grandchildren were coming tonight to help decorate the Christmas tree.

I had better get busy and make good choices on how I would spend the day. What chores would I do first? I certainly had plenty to do. I had been preparing menus and such for the family Christmas at my house this year.

Cleaning. That must be first on my list. I needed to clean and I could save decorating for last. The children would enjoy helping me decorate the tree. I was anxious to see their expressions as they rummage through the new decorations I bought this year. The final outcome will be quite a surprise since I was letting them make the choices for the tree. I thought to myself, 'I'd better quit daydreaming. There was no time to waste. I needed to stay focused on my chores.'

Just as I was finishing up the last of my chores, I heard the kids yelling as they ran through the door, "Mima, we're here! Let's decorate the tree," yells Nick. His greeting is followed by Destiny's, "I'm thirsty!" and Darius', "I'm hungry!"

I hugged them all and told them we were going to decorate the tree first; and then, we would have our usual hot cocoa and cookies as we read our Christmas book. This was our time together and something special we would do when they spent the night.

I had the children to sit by the fireplace so it would be easy dividing the ornaments. I then asked them to think about what Christmas meant to them and what they thought was the true meaning of Christmas. Darius raised his hand first; but, they all said they knew the answer. I let Darius answer first. What does Christmas mean to you, Darius? Darius gave me his answer and I was really surprised he didn't say 'getting presents.' I thought this would be a good time to tell them about their grandmothers and great-grandmothers, since they were the ones that taught me about Christmas. They taught me that it is not how much we give; but, how much love we put into giving to others.

I started with my mother-in-law, Grandma Weatherford-Climber. I told them how she didn't have lots of money so she would make beautiful quilts for Christmas gifts. Grandma Climber would use vegetables from her summer garden to can jars of vegetable soup. She would give the quilts and canned soup as Christmas gifts. She worked long and hard on the quilts. I remember her fingers would bleed. She would wrap them and keep going. She was on a time schedule. Grandma Climber had a very special gift. Not only were the gifts made with love, but, she also gave of herself, her time, and the substance of her life. I showed them the Christmas quilt she had made with Santa and his workshop. Grandma Climber had passed away before she was able to give it to the one for whom she had made it. One day Aunt Nita found it in her closet and she had the thought that Anna had wanted this quilt to go to Roni's new baby. It probably wasn't a coincidence, since, Roni had named her baby Nicholaus, after St. Nick.

He was better known as Santa Claus because he had the spirit of giving.

Now, color your own Santa's workshop.

I shared with them how my grandmother, Mimmie Lillis Mize, used to sit us in chairs in a row and read the Bible to us. We were too little to read; so, she would also tell us the different stories from the Bible. I'll never forget the one about the big fish that swallowed Jonah when he disobeyed the Lord. Mimmie wanted us to grow up and be strong in the Lord and obey His commandments. She taught me a scripture that has stayed with me for years.

John 3:15 –16 That whoever believes in him should not die, but have eternal life. For God so loved the world, that he gave his only begotten Son, that whosoever believeth in him should not perish, but have everlasting life.

My dad's mom, Mimmie Effie Wilkett, loved for the family to live close by so they could spend holidays together. She lived in a time when people would have to travel by covered wagons or by horses and that could take days of travel if they lived far apart. She loved cooking and having everyone at her house no matter how small her house was or how many would come.

My mom, Gladys Wilkett, was a school teacher of art, Spanish, and history. She was known as 'Nino' to her grandchildren. She loved to teach. Nino loved reading the Bible and finding hidden clues. She would share it with others through her paintings and teachings.

1. Mitten 2. Present 3. Bell 4. Star
5. (across) Snowflake 5. (down) Santa
6. Fireplace 7. Cookie 8. Snowman
9. Tree 10. Hat 11. Ball 12. Candle

I told the children they all have gifts and I wanted them to use them. I made them promise me, as cousins, they would always stay close to their family and love one another. I shared with them how their parents were close to their cousins at one time, but they let distance rob them of being close as adults.

Okay, enough about family because it's time to decorate the tree. The kids eagerly picked the ones they wanted to hang. There were crosses, angels, stars, a crown, peace, joy, a church, Mary, Joseph, and Baby Jesus.

Finally, the decorations were hung on the tree and it was time for baking and hot cocoa making. The children loved to help; maybe, because I also let them eat some cookie dough as we were putting the cookie dough on the pan to bake. The hot cocoa was ready so each one took mini marshmallows and dropped them one by one into their cup until their cups were filled to the top. The cookies were done, but, the chocolate chips needed to cool. As the cookies cooled, I told the children I wanted to share some teachings that Ninnie had sent me about Christmas.

I asked them if they knew why we cut down a tree and decorate it? No one had a clue. Long, long ago in Germany, there was a man named St. Boniface. He came across some godless people who were about to sacrifice a child at the base of a huge oak tree. Boniface quickly cut down the tree to prevent them from killing the child. In its place grew a fir tree. He then told everyone that this lovely evergreen, with its branches pointing toward heaven, signified peace, immortality and the dwelling place of God. Boniface believed it was a tree of the Christ child and a symbol of His promise of eternal life. It was also believed that evergreen trees warded off witches, ghosts, evil spirits and illnesses.*

The children were amazed at this story. My grandchildren never knew the importance of having a tree or decorating it. They were never taught the symbolism of the tree. I thought this was something they needed to know, as well as myself.

I asked them if they knew the importance of the star and its symbolism? I explained to them that the star placed on the tree represents Jesus' ministry, which was His teachings about salvation and Life. Each one of us is a star; because, we each have a gift or ministry given to us by God.

Well, the cookies are cooled and the kids can't wait! Oh, by the way, Darius' answer of what Christmas meant to him was 'giving.' The other two agreed. I, too, agree with Darius. Giving of yourself is more important than giving presents. The perfect gift is giving, the gift of love.

As my grandkids enjoyed the fruits of their labor – hot cocoa and chocolate chip cookies – we talked about their other cousins that would visit us on Christmas day. I had one more surprise for them. It was time to share with them my Christmas gift for their Papa Ronnie. I stepped into the bedroom and gathered up my gift. It was a little female English bulldog puppy. Ronnie had been very sick and I had read that pets were healing. I thought this would make the perfect gift for him. When I brought out the puppy, the children yelled, "Let me hold her!"

They took turns holding the puppy. Destiny asked, "What are you going to name her?"

I answered, "I am going to name her Dottie, which means Gift of God."

*(www.ewtn.com)

P.S. After the original writing of this book, I have been blessed with another grandchild, Hank William,.

Nick asked Mima to find stars for the cousins that couldn't be with us at Christmas, but they were with us in spirit. *Until a new day.*

CAN YOU FIND YOUR NAME IN THE PUZZLE?

DARIUS	DESTINY	JOSH	MINISTRY	BRANDON	CALEB ANDREW
CALEB	LOREN	JARRETT	ISABELLA	TEACHER	MCKENZIE
JACOB	MAKENNA	MILEY	PASTOR	TREE	NICHOLAUS
OLIVIA	EVELYN	HENRY	KEATON	JESUS	AMBROSIA
CIANNA	TRACE	GIVING	PEACE	LOVE	KYNZLEE
PAIGE	EMMA	ZACK	JAKE	ZAIDEN	DELANEY
CHLOE	ERIN	VIVIAN	ELI	HANK	SOPHIA
COOPER					

m	c	k	a	n	e	r	s	c	c	h	l	o	e	c	g	n	i	v	i	g	w	i	s	e
a	o	c	o	u	n	c	e	h	o	t	q	g	c	a	o	m	c	k	e	n	z	i	e	i
k	c	a	z	t	o	n	a	l	t	n	i	c	h	o	l	a	u	s	u	g	g	e	s	g
n	o	l	l	t	u	t	r	e	p	a	l	r	o	r	d	m	i	n	i	s	t	r	y	e
a	a	e	d	e	n	t	r	o	p	o	f	g	j	b	a	l	n	i	n	n	i	e	k	y
b	u	b	a	r	b	r	f	a	r	t	i	a	x	o	i	s	a	b	e	l	l	a	n	e
r	e	a	n	a	a	a	j	e	c	f	m	y	d	c	j	m	i	m	a	g	i	c	a	n
a	t	n	i	j	c	a	n	t	r	e	e	e	x	a	a	e	v	o	l	v	e	m	h	a
n	a	d	n	z	e	y	k	d	s	i	n	v	k	j	r	m	i	v	i	k	a	i	a	l
d	i	r	o	b	b	s	a	z	a	i	d	e	n	j	a	i	l	v	k	u	v	l	n	e
o	h	e	n	r	y	v	u	a	n	a	n	l	n	k	b	b	o	n	h	h	t	e	b	d
n	p	w	c	a	e	p	h	s	m	a	j	y	e	h	e	d	e	s	t	i	n	y	e	q
p	o	l	l	y	r	o	k	e	a	t	o	n	m	s	o	r	o	t	s	a	p	e	t	u
o	s	y	r	a	m	e	l	i	m	m	n	k	m	c	a	j	g	r	e	h	c	a	e	t
h	k	a	i	s	o	r	b	m	a	a	n	n	a	i	c	o	o	p	e	i	m	m	i	m

COLOR THE FAMILY

To God, the family is very important and He wants them to stay together. The mother is to nurture and the father is to train.

ACKNOWLEDGEMENT

In January 2016, I lost Dottie. I want to thank her for all the love, joy and laughter she brought to our family. She blessed me with 9 precious grandpuppies at the hardest time in my life. Dottie and her puppies have been the inspiration for my Christian children's books. She will always live on in my heart.

ABOUT THE AUTHOR

After a long illness, Connie Weatherford lost her husband, Ronnie, of almost 38 years in 2011. She thought about giving up the idea of writing Christian children's books, but, her husband's words of encouragement lives on in her heart.

The first book written by the author, *Dottie & Diego - A True Love Story,* is an actual true story of her life with Ronnie. It is paralleled through the story of her nine puppies. She raised English Bulldogs and called them her 'kids.'

This book is based on a true story as well. It is the prequel to her first book. The author's greatest desire is that her books will teach children the true love of God through the fruits of the Spirit, the love of a family, and the obedience to God and parents.

Dottie and her 9 pups

www.ingramcontent.com/pod-product-compliance
Lightning Source LLC
Chambersburg PA
CBHW041230040426
42444CB00002B/120

www.ingramcontent.com/pod-product-compliance
Lightning Source LLC
Chambersburg PA
CBHW081253040426
42453CB00014B/2401